Turning Points in History

THE McCARTHY HEARINGS

Nick Rebman

WWW.APEXEDITIONS.COM

Copyright © 2025 by Apex Editions, Mendota Heights, MN 55120. All rights reserved. No part of this book may be reproduced or utilized in any form or by any means without written permission from the publisher.

Apex is distributed by North Star Editions:
sales@northstareditions.com | 888-417-0195

Produced for Apex by Red Line Editorial.

Photographs ©: AP Images, cover, 1, 16–17, 24–25, 34–35, 58; Keystone-France/Gamma-Keystone/Getty Images, 4–5; Library of Congress, 6–7, 10–11; National Archives, 8–9; Arthur S. Siegel/Library of Congress, 12–13; Shutterstock Images, 14–15, 46–47; Marion S. Trikosko/Library of Congress, 19, 52–53; Corporal Peter McDonald/US Marine Corps, 20–21; Bettmann/Getty Images, 22–23, 26–27, 30–31, 32–33, 40–41, 42–43, 44–45, 49; Herbert K. White/AP Images, 28–29; iStockphoto, 36–37; Bernard Gotfryd/Library of Congress, 38–39; American Stock Archive/Archive Photos/Getty Images, 50–51; Bebeto Matthews/AP Images, 54–55; Chuck Kennedy/KRT/Newscom, 56–57

Library of Congress Control Number: 2024943630

ISBN
979-8-89250-464-5 (hardcover)
979-8-89250-480-5 (paperback)
979-8-89250-510-9 (ebook pdf)
979-8-89250-496-6 (hosted ebook)

Printed in the United States of America
Mankato, MN
012025

NOTE TO PARENTS AND EDUCATORS

Apex books are designed to build literacy skills in striving readers. Exciting, high-interest content attracts and holds readers' attention. The text is carefully leveled to allow students to achieve success quickly.

TABLE OF CONTENTS

Chapter 1
RUINED REPUTATION 4

Chapter 2
RED SCARE 8

Story Spotlight
HOOVER'S FBI 18

Chapter 3
THE FEAR SPREADS 21

Chapter 4
HEARINGS BEGIN 30

Chapter 5
TURNING POINT 40

Story Spotlight
JOSEPH NYE WELCH 48

Chapter 6
LEGACY 50

TIMELINE • 59
COMPREHENSION QUESTIONS • 60
GLOSSARY • 62
TO LEARN MORE • 63
ABOUT THE AUTHOR • 63
INDEX • 64

Chapter 1

RUINED REPUTATION

In April 1953, Senator Joseph McCarthy called a hearing. He questioned Theodore Kaghan. Kaghan worked for the US government. McCarthy thought Kaghan was a Communist. Many US leaders opposed that political party.

Theodore Kaghan (center) worked in Austria for the United States. He also helped run an anti-Communist newspaper.

McCarthy asked question after question. Was Kaghan a Communist? Did he believe similar ideas? Did he know any Communists? McCarthy even brought up plays Kaghan had written. He asked if the plays sounded Communist.

McCarthy made Kaghan appear disloyal to the United States. He ruined Kaghan's reputation. As a result, Kaghan lost his job.

US FREEDOMS

The US Constitution lists people's rights. People are free to believe what they want. Even unpopular ideas are protected. People can join any political party. It is legal to disagree with the government. That does not make a person disloyal.

Joseph McCarthy's work against Communism cost thousands of government workers their jobs.

Chapter 2

RED SCARE

Joseph McCarthy held many hearings similar to the one with Theodore Kaghan. These hearings took place in the early years of the Cold War (1947–1991). The United States and the Soviet Union were enemies. They did not fight each other directly. However, they had strong disagreements.

The United States and the Soviet Union built powerful weapons. The two countries came very close to fighting each other.

The Soviet Union formed in 1922. Vladimir Lenin was its first leader.

Soviet leaders supported Communism. This system has a few main ideas. The public owns most property. Also, the government controls most businesses.

The Soviet Union's government had a one-party system. The Communist Party was in charge. Other parties were not allowed.

MAJOR DIFFERENCES

US leaders supported capitalism. In this system, individuals own property. Individuals control businesses, too. US leaders also supported democracy. People can choose from more than one party.

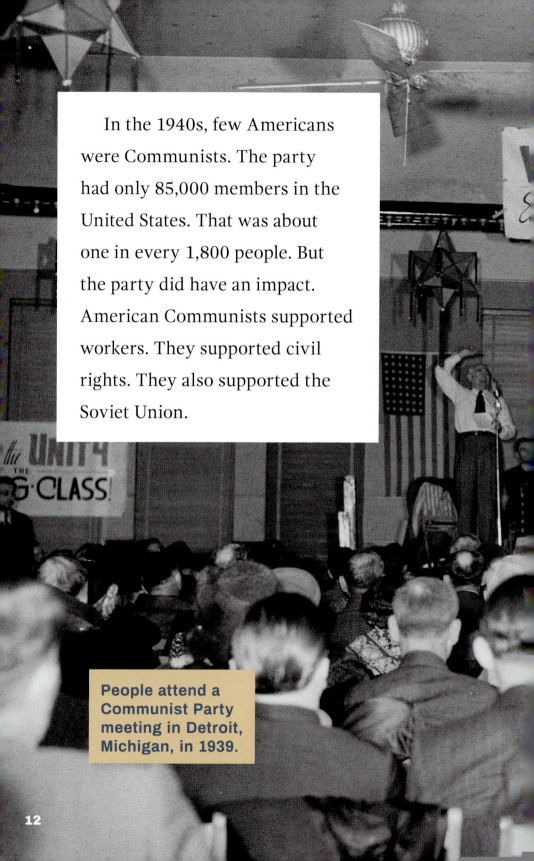

In the 1940s, few Americans were Communists. The party had only 85,000 members in the United States. That was about one in every 1,800 people. But the party did have an impact. American Communists supported workers. They supported civil rights. They also supported the Soviet Union.

People attend a Communist Party meeting in Detroit, Michigan, in 1939.

In the late 1940s, US leaders had many fears about Communism. They feared it would spread to other countries. They also feared it would spread within the United States. So, US leaders saw American Communists as a danger. This period became known as the Second Red Scare.

FIRST RED SCARE

In 1917, Communists took over Russia. Some Americans worried that a similar event could happen in the United States. This fear led to the First Red Scare. US law enforcement made thousands of arrests. They targeted Communists. They also targeted people who they thought had similar beliefs.

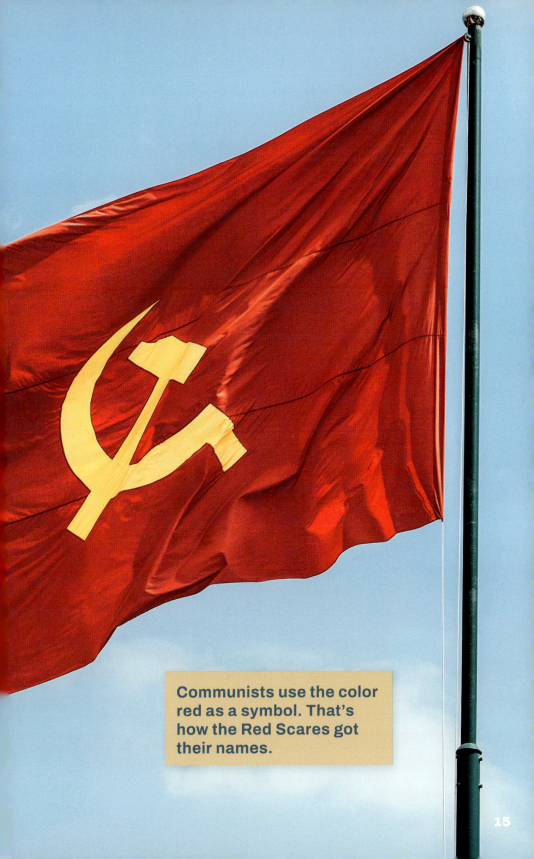

Communists use the color red as a symbol. That's how the Red Scares got their names.

Harry S. Truman was the US president when the Second Red Scare began. He tried to remove Communists from positions of power. In 1947, he set up loyalty tests. Government workers had to swear they opposed Communism. Similar tests soon spread to non-government jobs.

BLACKLISTING

In 1947, US lawmakers looked into the movie business. They asked workers if they were Communists. Some people refused to answer. Movie studios assumed these people were Communists. As a result, they weren't given work. This idea is known as blacklisting.

US law enforcement sent 10 movie workers to prison for not answering questions about Communism.

Story Spotlight

HOOVER'S FBI

The FBI is the US government's law enforcement agency. It helped Truman during the Second Red Scare. The FBI tried to find Communists. It broke many laws trying to get information. For example, the FBI secretly listened to people's phone calls. It opened people's mail. It broke into people's offices.

J. Edgar Hoover led the FBI. He said people who opposed his methods were helping Communism spread.

The FBI accused many people of being Communists. Often, the FBI did not say how it got this information. As a result, people could not defend themselves.

J. Edgar Hoover led the FBI for nearly 48 years.

The United States helped South Korea in the Korean War. The US government wanted to stop North Korea from spreading Communism.

Chapter 3

THE FEAR SPREADS

Communists gained control of China in 1949. A year later, Communist forces invaded South Korea. That set off the Korean War (1950–1953). These events increased US fear of Communism. Americans saw that it was spreading.

Alger Hiss worked for the US government. In 1948, he was accused of spying for the Soviet Union. And in 1950, he was found guilty of lying in court. The trial had a big effect. More people thought Communist spies were in the US government.

THE ROSENBERGS

Julius and Ethel Rosenberg were American Communists. In 1950, the two were arrested. They were charged with spying. A jury found them guilty. They had given the Soviet Union US secrets. The Rosenbergs were put to death in 1953.

Alger Hiss spent nearly four years in jail.

Joseph McCarthy was a US senator. He paid attention to the Hiss trial. A few weeks later, he gave a speech. McCarthy claimed to have an important list. The list named 205 Communists. He said they worked in the US government. And they were spying for the Soviet Union.

SEARCHING FOR AN ISSUE

McCarthy won his Senate seat in 1946. At first, few Americans knew who he was. McCarthy wanted an issue that would help him win reelection. He found it when he started talking about Communism.

Media sold many newspapers by talking about McCarthy. That helped make McCarthy famous.

McCarthy didn't share his list. He didn't give any names. And he didn't offer any proof for his claims. But he quickly became famous. McCarthy gained lots of supporters. They liked that he opposed Communism.

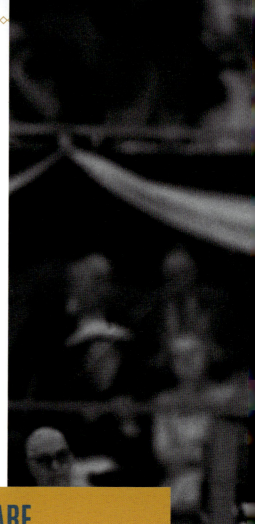

THE LAVENDER SCARE

McCarthy linked Communism with being gay. He also made other homophobic claims. They were all false. But many people believed him. Thousands of gay workers were fired. These actions became known as the Lavender Scare.

McCarthy's fame quickly made him powerful within his political party.

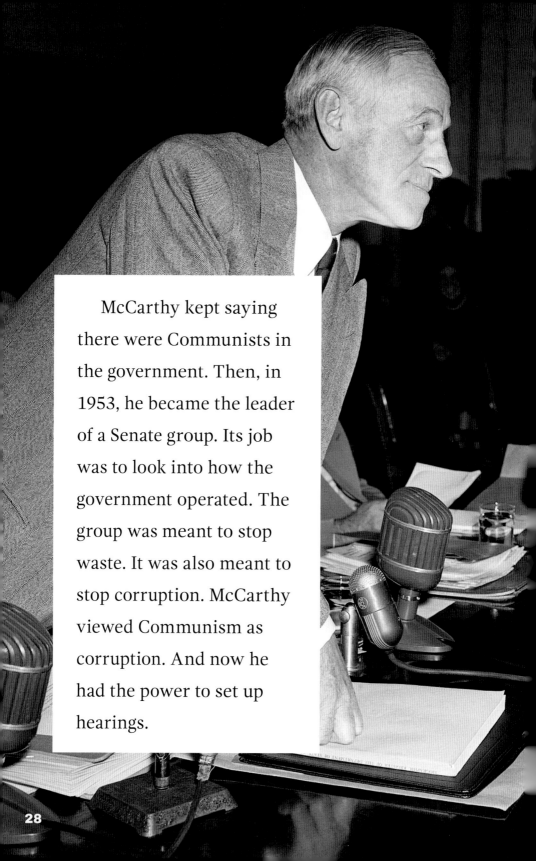

McCarthy kept saying there were Communists in the government. Then, in 1953, he became the leader of a Senate group. Its job was to look into how the government operated. The group was meant to stop waste. It was also meant to stop corruption. McCarthy viewed Communism as corruption. And now he had the power to set up hearings.

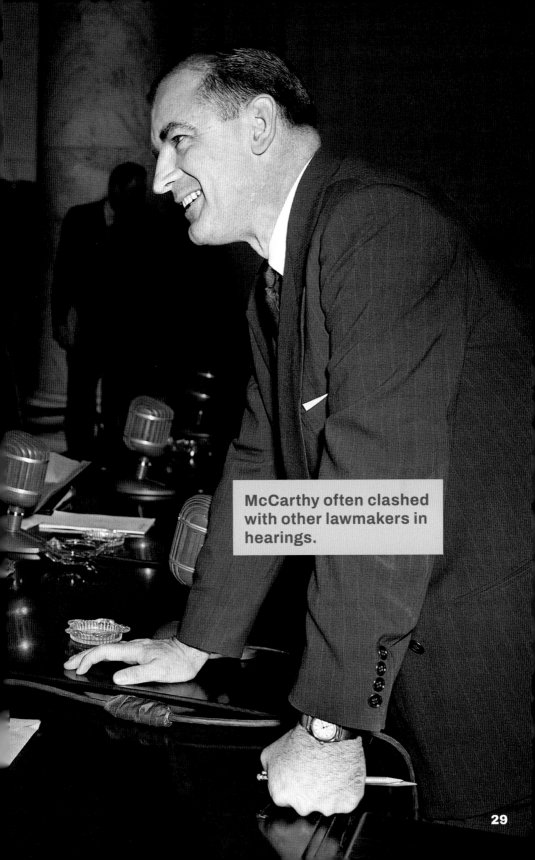

McCarthy often clashed with other lawmakers in hearings.

Chapter 4

HEARINGS BEGIN

Starting in 1953, McCarthy held many hearings. He called in hundreds of people. They had to answer his questions. McCarthy's first target was Voice of America. This was a radio station. The US government ran it. McCarthy claimed some of its workers were Communists.

Between 1953 and 1954, McCarthy held 169 hearings.

McCarthy pressed Voice of America workers for answers. He asked if they knew any Communists. He did not find any. Even so, the hearings created fear. One worker worried that McCarthy was going to call him in. So, the worker took his own life.

ACTING ALONE

McCarthy gave little notice for many of his hearings. He also held many hearings in odd places. They were not easy for other senators to get to. So, McCarthy was often the only senator at the hearings. There was no one to oppose him.

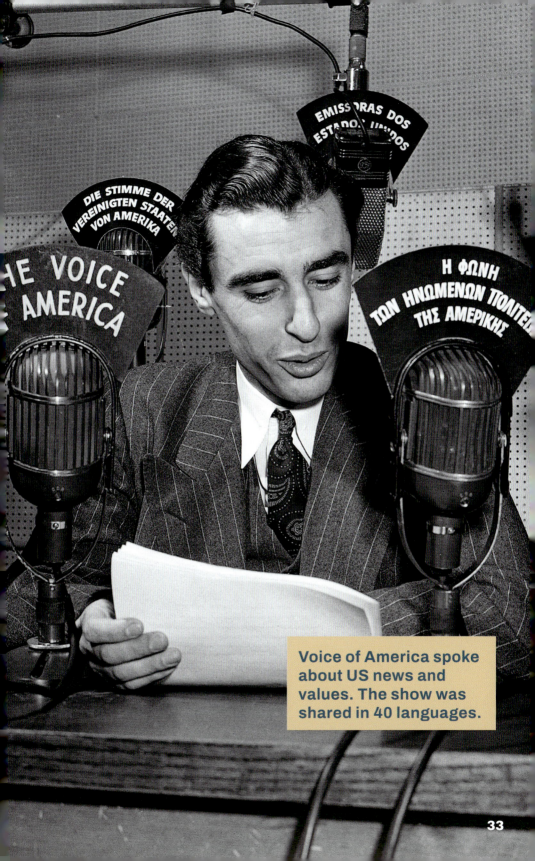

Voice of America spoke about US news and values. The show was shared in 40 languages.

Next, McCarthy focused on writers. For example, he called in Langston Hughes. Hughes was a well-known poet. McCarthy's team asked Hughes if he was a Communist. They asked over and over again. They often interrupted Hughes. This type of questioning was common.

BOOK BURNING

The US government has libraries around the world. In the 1950s, these libraries got caught up in the Red Scare. Many pulled certain books off their shelves. They didn't want people to read books by Communists. In a few cases, the libraries even burned books.

Writer Langston Hughes answers questions before McCarthy's Senate committee in 1953.

We the People

Article 1

People have a right to not answer questions. It is protected by the US Constitution.

5th Ame

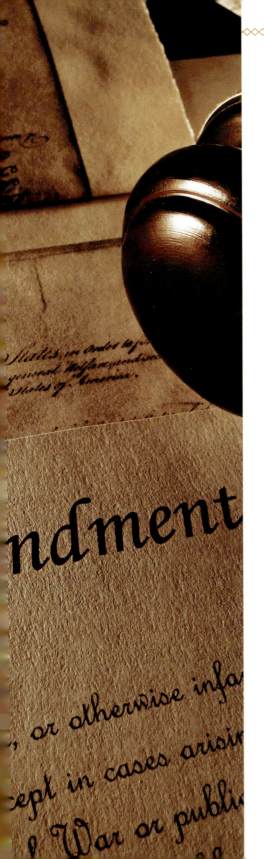

After that, McCarthy went after college professors. Many professors refused to say whether they knew any Communists. That was their right. But McCarthy said they shouldn't stay silent. He said it showed that they supported Communism. As a result, some professors lost their jobs.

Many lawmakers disagreed with McCarthy's methods. But most were afraid to oppose him. They thought it would make them look weak on Communism. They wanted to show they were keeping the country safe.

SPEAKING OUT

Margaret Chase Smith was the only female senator at the time. She was also the first senator to speak out against McCarthy. Smith believed McCarthy was being unfair. She said all Americans had the right to believe whatever they wanted.

Margaret Chase Smith served in the US Senate for 24 years.

Chapter 5
TURNING POINT

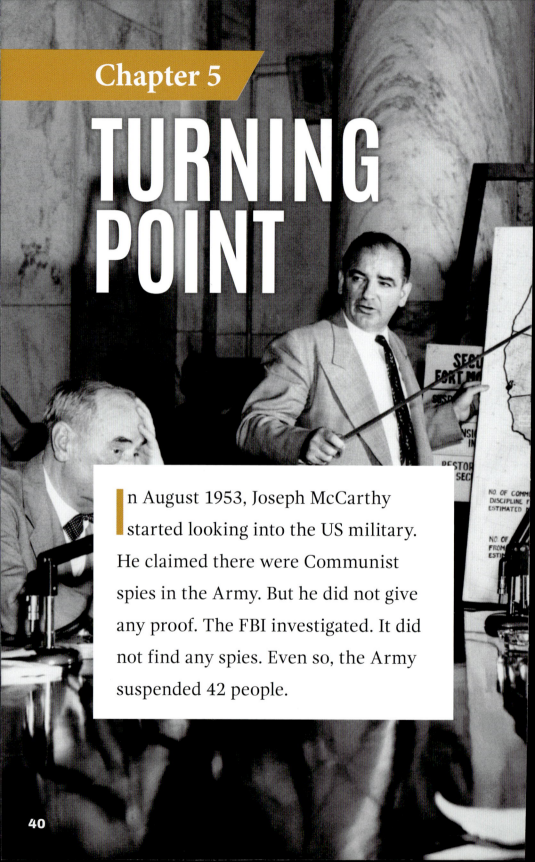

In August 1953, Joseph McCarthy started looking into the US military. He claimed there were Communist spies in the Army. But he did not give any proof. The FBI investigated. It did not find any spies. Even so, the Army suspended 42 people.

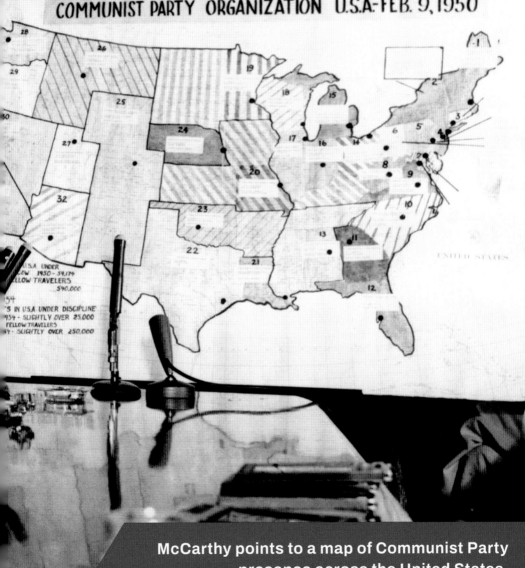

McCarthy points to a map of Communist Party presence across the United States.

McCarthy cut a person out of a photo to support his false claims.

In March 1954, new hearings began. This time, senators looked into McCarthy. They asked about his claims against the Army. McCarthy spoke as much as he could. He focused on an Army dentist. McCarthy said the dentist had Communist ties. McCarthy damaged the man's reputation. People threw rocks at his home. The dentist also took his name off his business. And his wife stepped down from her work.

Edward R. Murrow had a radio and TV show. He talked about the news and the spread of false information.

The Army hearings were on TV. Millions of Americans watched. They saw the way McCarthy made claims without proof. They saw how he interrupted people. And they saw how he insulted people. Many people viewed McCarthy as a bully.

The hearings were the height of his fame. But they came at a cost. They hurt his own reputation.

THE POWER OF TV

In the early 1950s, TV was still new. Many people paid attention to it. Reporter Edward R. Murrow spoke out about McCarthy. He explained how McCarthy was being unfair. Murrow helped shift public opinion.

In December 1954, senators took a vote. They voted to censure McCarthy. That meant the Senate did not approve of his actions. McCarthy had behaved poorly. And he had broken the Senate's rules. After the censure, McCarthy had much less power.

BANNING COMMUNISM

In August 1954, Congress passed a law. It banned the Communist Party. This law went against the US Constitution. However, the law was rarely used. And later, lawmakers changed it.

The Senate meets in the US Capitol building in Washington, DC.

Story Spotlight

JOSEPH NYE WELCH

Joseph Nye Welch was a lawyer for the Army. He spoke at the hearings. McCarthy made claims about another lawyer on Welch's team. He said the lawyer supported a Communist group. Welch asked McCarthy not to hurt the lawyer's reputation. But McCarthy didn't stop. So, Welch interrupted McCarthy. He said, "Have you no sense of decency, sir?"

Welch had stood up to McCarthy. People at the hearing clapped. Millions more watched on TV. After that, McCarthy lost many supporters.

Joseph Nye Welch was very calm compared to McCarthy's harsh methods.

Chapter 6

LEGACY

Joseph McCarthy died in 1957. However, the word *McCarthyism* lived on. It describes what McCarthy did to many people. It means questioning people's loyalty without giving proof. It also involves unfair methods of questioning. And it involves trying to keep opponents silent.

Even after McCarthy's hearings, many people still protested Communism.

The fear of Communism had decreased by the 1960s. However, McCarthyism continued. US leaders went after other left-leaning groups. The government illegally spied on civil rights leaders. One target was Martin Luther King Jr.

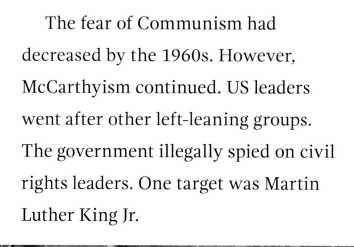

LEFT AND RIGHT

Communism is a left-wing belief. People on the left tend to support large changes. They say the government should play a strong role in helping people. People on the right often call for less government. They also focus on tradition. Many support following authority, too.

The FBI targeted many Black civil rights leaders in the 1960s.

Terrorists attacked the United States on September 11, 2001. Many people worried about more attacks after that. Similar to the 1950s, it was a time of fear. Lawmakers made it easier for the government to spy on people. Some lawmakers opposed the idea. They were accused of being weak on terrorism. Some people said those charges were an example of McCarthyism.

TARGETING MUSLIMS

The September 11 terrorists were Muslims. Afterward, the US government spied on many Muslim Americans. This went against their rights. The US government said it was for safety. But many people said that was a false trade-off.

Many Muslims spoke out against being unfairly targeted by the US government.

McCarthyism still exists today. It is usually not about Communism. But some people still make false charges. Their claims are not backed by facts. Instead, they try to make people afraid. And they try to hurt the careers of their opponents. Many lawmakers go along with them. They don't want to seem weak.

In 2003, the Senate released the records from the McCarthy hearings. One senator said she hoped it would help avoid similar situations.

TIMELINE

OCTOBER 1917 — Communists take control of Russia. They later form the Soviet Union.

OCTOBER 1, 1949 — Communists take control of China.

JANUARY 21, 1950 — Alger Hiss is found guilty, leading many Americans to believe that Communist spies are working in the US government.

FEBRUARY 9, 1950 — Senator Joseph McCarthy claims to have a list of 205 Communists working in the US government.

FEBRUARY 13, 1953 — McCarthy leads a series of hearings looking into Voice of America.

AUGUST 31, 1953 — McCarthy starts looking into the US military.

JUNE 9, 1954 — Army lawyer Joseph Nye Welch stands up to McCarthy during a hearing. The public begins to see McCarthy as a bully.

DECEMBER 2, 1954 — The Senate votes to censure McCarthy. After that, McCarthy loses much of his power.

COMPREHENSION QUESTIONS

Write your answers on a separate piece of paper.

1. Write a paragraph that explains the main ideas of Chapter 3.

2. Do you think other senators should have done more to stop Joseph McCarthy? Why or why not?

3. Who set up loyalty tests in 1947?

   A. Harry S. Truman
   B. Margaret Chase Smith
   C. Alger Hiss

4. When did McCarthy give his first speech about Communists?

   A. 1946
   B. 1950
   C. 1954

5. What does **assumed** mean in this book?

*They asked workers if they were Communists. Some people refused to answer. Movie studios **assumed** these people were Communists.*

    A. started a new type of work

    B. believed what people said

    C. believed something without proof

6. What does **investigated** mean in this book?

*The FBI **investigated**. It did not find any spies.*

    A. sent people to prison

    B. spied on other countries

    C. tried to find an answer

Answer key on page 64.

GLOSSARY

accused
Charged a person with doing wrong or illegal things.

civil rights
Rights that protect people's freedom and equality.

Constitution
The document that lays out the basic beliefs and laws of the United States.

corruption
Dishonest or illegal acts, often by powerful people.

disloyal
Not supporting one's country.

hearing
A meeting in which lawmakers ask questions and gather information.

homophobic
Involving hatred or mistreatment of people because of their sexuality.

political party
A group that has specific ideas about how the government should be run.

reputation
The beliefs that the public has about a person.

suspended
Stopped someone from being able to work for a certain period of time.

terrorists
People who attack and scare others to reach their goals.

TO LEARN MORE
BOOKS

Rossiter, Brienna. *The Korean War*. Mendota Heights, MN: Focus Readers, 2024.

Stratton, Connor. *The Cold War*. Mendota Heights, MN: Focus Readers, 2024.

Walker, Tracy Sue. *Spotlight on Russia*. Minneapolis: Lerner Publications, 2024.

ONLINE RESOURCES

Visit **www.apexeditions.com** to find links and resources related to this title.

ABOUT THE AUTHOR

Nick Rebman is a writer and editor who lives in Minnesota.

INDEX

Army, 40, 43, 45, 48

blacklisting, 16
book burning, 34

censure, 46
China, 21
Cold War, 8
Constitution, 6, 46

FBI, 18, 40
First Red Scare, 14

Hiss, Alger, 22, 24
Hoover, J. Edgar, 18
Hughes, Langston, 34

Kaghan, Theodore, 4, 6, 8
King, Martin Luther, Jr., 52
Korean War, 21

Lavender Scare, 26

McCarthyism, 50, 52, 54, 56
Murrow, Edward R., 45
Muslim Americans, 54

professors, 37

Rosenberg, Ethel, 22
Rosenberg, Julius, 22

Second Red Scare, 14, 16, 18, 34
September 11, 54
Smith, Margaret Chase, 38
Soviet Union, 8, 11–12, 22, 24
spying, 22, 24, 40, 52, 54

Truman, Harry S., 16, 18
TV, 45, 48

Voice of America, 30, 32

Welch, Joseph Nye, 48

ANSWER KEY:

1. Answers will vary; 2. Answers will vary; 3. A; 4. B; 5. C; 6. C